Bedtime Prayers
TO READ TOGETHER

A gift for:

_____

From:

_____

Copyright © 2011 Hallmark Licensing, Inc.

Published by Hallmark Gift Books,
a division of Hallmark Cards, Inc.,
Kansas City, MO 64141
Visit us on the Web at www.Hallmark.com.

Editor: Chelsea Fogleman
Art Director: Kevin Swanson
Designer: Brian Pilachowski
Production Artist: Dan Horton

ISBN: 978-1-59530-421-6
BOK1185

Printed and bound in China
AUG11

Bedtime Prayers
TO READ TOGETHER

WRITTEN AND SELECTED BY Diana Manning

Introduction

Saying your prayers is just talking to God—and you can talk to Him about anything! You can ask Him for things, thank Him for things, and come to Him with everything you're wondering about. He cares about you and always loves the times you spend together.

Here's a book of bedtime prayers you can read with someone before you go to sleep at night. Maybe it will help you think of new things to talk to God about.

And when your prayers are over and it's time to go to sleep, your special angel night light will shine to remind you that God is watching over you with love . . . at bedtime and always.

Five little angels round my bed.
One to the foot and one to the head.
One to sing and one to pray,
And one to carry my cares away.

Thanks for today, God—
I had a good time.
In all my best memories,
today's going to shine!

I went somewhere special
where I got to see
a lot of new things
that were so fun for me.

When I go to sleep at night,
You pull the darkness over me
like a soft, warm blanket.
You light the stars
to twinkle over me,
and You sing me to sleep
with the wind.
All night long,
You're watching over me
with love.
And I know I'm safe
in Your arms.

God bless all those that I love,
God bless all those that love me.
God bless all those that love those that I love
and all those that love those who love me.

New England Sampler

Dear God,
May You bless me
in big ways and small ways,
front ways and sideways,
short ways and tall ways . . .
and shine Your love on me
at bedtime and always!

Jesus,
Bless me as I grow.
Bless all of me
from head to toe.
Bless my smile,
and bless my frown,
Eyebrows that go
up and down.
Bless my arms
with hugs to share—
Bless the hands
I fold in prayer.
Bless my feet
so I'll stand strong
close by Your side
my whole life long!

Thanks, God,
for the chance to have fun today.
I smiled so hard
that my face almost hurt!
But still, it felt really, really good.
I bet You like to see kids smiling
and feeling happy
because You love us so much!

Hold on to what is good,
even if it's just a small, round pebble.
Hold on to who you are,
even if it means being like a tree
that stands alone.
Hold on to what is right,
even if you must travel a long road
to get there.
Hold on to the hand of God . . .
because He's always holding on to you.

Based on a Pueblo Indian Prayer

Thank You, God,
for giving me friends
to play with,
to laugh with,
and have all kinds of fun with.

Help me, God,
to be a good friend myself . . .
to share,
to care,
and be kind.

The Lord is good to me,
and so I thank the Lord
for giving me the things I need,
the sun and the rain and the appleseed.
The Lord is good to me.

John Chapman ("Johnny Appleseed"),
Planter of Orchards

Today was a good day, Lord.
I had a lot of fun.
I learned new things
I didn't know before—
new words to say,
new games to play,
new things that I can do—
and every day I'm learning more and more.

14

Lord, You're my shepherd.
You give me everything I need.
You lead me like a little lamb
to green fields where I can rest
beside quiet waters.
You guide me in the right paths.
You keep me from all harm.
You're so good to me,
and I'm glad I can live
in Your home with You
forever!

Based on Psalm 23

Now I lay me down to sleep,
I pray the Lord my soul to keep.
Guard me, Jesus, through the night
And wake me with the morning light.

You made the earth
and saw that it was very, very good—
now help us to take care of it
the way we know we should.

Help us keep Your rivers clean,
your forests standing tall,
and show us how to care
for all Your creatures, great and small.

We want to keep the earth
the way You made it from the start—
all fresh and green and beautiful,
so help us do our part!

I'm so glad I'm part of a family
who loves me and takes care of me.
And I'm glad I'm part
of Your family, too, God.
Help me to remember
that all the children in the world
are precious in Your sight.
Help me to remember
they're all my brothers and sisters in You!

Summer, winter,
spring, and fall.
Thanks for the seasons—
I love them all!

Dear God,
 I try to follow You
and do the best I can,
but when I make mistakes,
You're always there to understand—
'cause You know all about me
and what's there inside my heart,
the way You always have
since You've been with me from the start.

Dear God,
You take good care of me
and always fill my tummy.
So thank You for my food today—
it tasted really yummy!

Dear God,
Be good to me—
the sea is so wide,
and my boat is so small.

The Breton Fisherman's Prayer from France

You know the plans You have for me . . .
that's what Your Word has said.
They're plans for good and hopeful things
and happiness ahead.

Each day looks even brighter,
for my future's in Your hands—
Thank You, God, for blessing me
with special, lifelong plans!

Based on Jeremiah 29:11

Dear God,
I have so many questions for You.
But You don't seem to mind.
I think You know
that's just the way kids are.

And even though I don't always
get the answers right away,
it's nice to get to talk to You awhile
and know You're listening.

Thank You, God, for animals,
the creatures in the woods,
the bunnies, birds, and woolly worms
around my neighborhood.

And thanks for my stuffed animals—
I love to hug them tight.
They're cuddly, cozy friends
who keep me company all night!

"Love your neighbor as yourself."
Sometimes it's hard to do, Lord.
Help me to forgive
when someone hurts my feelings.
And help me say I'm sorry
when I've hurt someone else.
Help me find new ways
to be kind each day.

Dear God,
You're good at making stuff,
like fuzzy bumblebees,
rainbows, rocks, and lily pads,
and starfish in the sea.

With my crayons, glue, and scissors,
I like to make stuff, too—
because I am Your child,
I must have gotten that from You!

Dear Jesus,
You said
to let the little children
come to You—
so each day,
when I want to pray,
that's what I'm going to do.

You took the children
in Your arms,
and then You blessed them, too—
Lord, keep me in Your arms
so I'll be blessed
my whole life through.

God,
You keep me safe
in all kinds of weather . . .
through thunder and lightning,
the wind, and the rain.
And afterward,
You paint your rainbow in the sky
to remind me
You're here with me always!

May the winds blow warm
upon your home.
May God
bless all who live inside.
May your moccasins
make happy tracks
in many snows,
and may rainbows
always touch your shoulder.

Based on a Cherokee Prayer Blessing

Thanks for listening when I pray
and help me listen, too.
So I can hear Your quiet ways
of saying "I love you."

Dear God,
You give the flowers of the field
their colorful clothes.
You give the birds of the air
plenty of food to eat.
So I know You'll always
take good care of me, too,
and give me all the things I need.
Thank You, God!

Based on Matthew 6:25-33

Dear Lord,
Please take care of us together
and help us work together
for the good of all people.
Amen

Based on a Prayer from India

Day by day, dear Lord, of Thee
three things I pray:
to see Thee more clearly,
love Thee more dearly,
follow Thee more nearly,
day by day.

St. Richard of Chichester

Dear God, You care for me every day.
Help me remember these words I can pray:
Lord, I'm going to hold steady on to You,
and You've got to see me through!

Based on Words by Harriet Tubman

Jesus loves me,
this I know.
And He'll bless me
as I grow.
He's been with me
from the start,
He'll always keep me
in His heart.

My family's like a circle,
holding hands and standing strong,
Sharing happy times together—
it's the place where I belong.

Your love's a circle, too, Lord,
like two arms surrounding me—
With no end and no beginning,
it's the nicest place to be!

For each new morning with its light,
For rest and shelter of the night,
For health and food,
For love and friends,
For everything Thy goodness sends.

Ralph Waldo Emerson

God made me unique—
I'm one of a kind.
Out of all of the millions
Of people I see,
There's nobody else
With my very same smile—
It's kind of nice knowing
There's only one me!

May the doors to our home
always be open to friends and neighbors.

May our windows
show us the beauty of the world outside.

May our roof remind us
of the way You shelter us
with Your love, Lord.

And may all those
who live inside
be truly blessed.

Dear God,
When You invented laughing,
it was a very good idea.
Because I got to laugh a lot today,
and it sure was fun!
Thank You, God.

Dear God,
Lots of people
need help with things,
and I was a good helper today.
As I grow taller, smarter,
and stronger each day,
show me new ways
I can help
when somebody needs me!

Bless our pets, Lord,
cats and dogs,
turtles, hamsters,
fish and frogs,
bless each whisker,
shell, and scale—
bless them all
from snout to tail!
They'll always be
such loyal friends,
So thank You, Lord—
Rrfff! Rrfff! Amen!

All things bright and beautiful,
all creatures great and small,
all things wise and wonderful,
the Lord God made them all.

Each little flower that opens,
each little bird that sings,
He made their glowing colors,
He made their tiny wings.

The purple-headed mountain,
the river running by,
the sunset, and the morning
that brightens up the sky.

Cecil Frances Alexander

May my mouth praise You.
May my ears hear Your words.
May my feet follow faithfully in Your footsteps.
Lord, may I always do Your will.

Based on a Japanese prayer

Lord, make me somebody

who shares Your spirit of peace.

Where there's anger,

let me spread love.

Where there are hurt feelings,

let me say "I'm sorry."

Where there is doubt,

let me help others to believe.

Where there is fear,

let me be brave.

Where there is darkness,

let me shine like a light.

Where there is sadness,

let me help people find their smiles again.

Based on Prayer of St. Francis of Assisi

God,
You made me
when I was just a baby,
so You really know me
and everything about me!
You planned all my days for me,
way into the future.
You're always thinking of me—
and when I wake up,
You're still going to be with me.

Based on Psalm 139:13-18

Jesus, You're my shepherd,
and I'm Your little lamb—
so here's a prayer to tell You
how very glad I am!

I hope I dream sweet dreams tonight
of sailing on a breeze,
drifting on a sailboat cloud
high above the trees—
dreams of playing hide-and-seek
and catching lightning bugs,
dreams that taste like lemonade,
dreams that feel like hugs.
I want to dream sweet dreams tonight,
Lord, this is what I pray—
please help me go to sleep
and dream sweet dreams
till break of day.

Dear God,
Bless all the kids around the world.
Bless the ones who sleep in huts,
the ones who carry water,
and the ones who harvest rice.
Bless the ones who help care
for their brothers and sisters.
Bless us all . . .
and keep us all in Your hands,
every one.

Thank You, Lord, for giving me
a soft and snuggly bed—
it feels so nice to have a place
to lay my sleepy head.

If you have enjoyed reading
these bedtime prayers,
we would love to hear from you.

Please send your comments to:
Hallmark Book Feedback
P.O. Box 419034
Mail Drop 215
Kansas City, MO 64141

Or e-mail us at:
booknotes@hallmark.com